LAW
DISABILITY BENEFITS

A Comprehensive Guide to Applying for Disability Benefits through the
Social Security Administration

Realize your constitutional right with qualified help

Maria Gonzalez

Table Of Contents

Introduction:

Welcome to "A Comprehensive Guide to Applying for Disability Benefits through the Social Security Administration." If you or a loved one are facing the challenges of a disability that impacts your ability to work, you're not alone. Navigating the process of applying for disability benefits can be complex and overwhelming, but this guide is here to simplify and demystify the journey.

Our aim is to provide you with a comprehensive roadmap that will lead you through each step of the application process, from understanding the basics of disability benefits to receiving the support you deserve. Applying for disability benefits is not only about financial assistance; it's about securing a lifeline that can help you maintain stability during a difficult time.

In this guide, we will break down the eligibility criteria, documentation requirements, and the various types of disability benefits offered by the Social Security Administration. We'll guide you through the process of gathering essential information, choosing the right program based on your circumstances, and navigating the application itself. Furthermore, we'll equip you with strategies for compiling strong medical evidence, presenting your work history, and dealing with possible denials.

The journey to securing disability benefits may not always be straightforward, but it's important to remember that you have rights, resources, and options. This guide is designed to empower you with knowledge and confidence so that you can advocate for yourself effectively throughout the application process.

Whether you're just starting to explore the possibility of applying for disability benefits or you're in the midst of a complex appeals process, this guide is here to support you. By the time you reach the end, you'll have a solid understanding of the process, potential challenges, and strategies for success.

Remember, you are not alone in this journey. This guide is a tool to help you navigate the path to securing the benefits you deserve. Let's embark on this journey together, one step at a time.

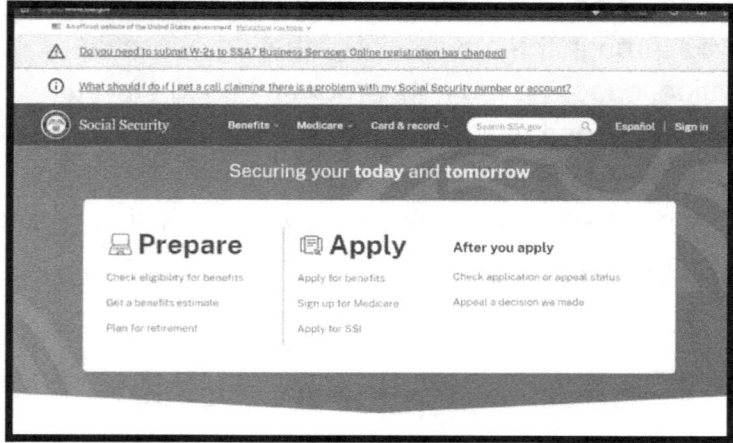

Chapter 1: Understanding Disability Benefits

When faced with a disability that affects your ability to work, understanding your options and the support available to you is crucial. Disability benefits provided by the Social Security Administration (SSA) can offer financial assistance and a safety net during these challenging times. In this chapter, we will delve into the fundamentals of disability benefits, eligibility criteria, and the different types of benefits offered.

1.1 Defining Disability Benefits

Disability benefits, offered through the SSA, are intended to provide financial assistance to individuals who are unable to work due to a disabling medical condition. These benefits are designed to help maintain a certain level of financial stability and improve the overall quality of life for those who are unable to engage in substantial gainful activity due to their health condition.

1.2 Who Is Eligible?

To qualify for disability benefits from the SSA, you need to meet specific eligibility criteria. The primary criterion is demonstrating that you have a medically determinable impairment that prevents you from engaging in substantial gainful activity (SGA). Substantial gainful activity refers to work that provides a certain level of income, which may change from year to year.

1.3 The SSA's Definition of Disability

It's important to note that the SSA has a specific definition of disability. According to the SSA, you are considered disabled if:

- You cannot perform work that you did before.
- The SSA determines that you cannot adjust to other work because of your medical condition(s).
- Your disability has lasted or is expected to last for at least one year, or it is expected to result in death.

1.4 Different Types of Disability Benefits

The SSA offers two main types of disability benefit programs: Social Security Disability Insurance (SSDI) and Supplemental Security Income (SSI).

1.4.1 Social Security Disability Insurance (SSDI)

SSDI is designed for individuals who have a significant work history and have paid Social Security taxes. To qualify for SSDI, you typically need to have accumulated a certain number of work credits based on your age and work history. The amount of your benefit is determined by your average lifetime earnings covered by Social Security. It is typically 40 credits over the last 10 years. If you have worked 5 out of the last 10 years you should be eligible. Keep in mind that if you stop working for five years, your credits will expire and make you ineligible.

For example, Sarah stopped working in 2015, so her working credits expirec in 2020 which means unless she became disabled and sought out medical treatment anywhere from 2015 to 2020, she would no longer qualify for SSDI. To be eligible for SSDI, you need to be a born citizen of the United States or you need to at least hold a green card from USCIS. If you are eligible for SSDI, you can see the estimated amount you would receive if you were to be found disabled by making an account on SSA.gov which will allow you to see your earnings record. The earnings record will show all the years you worked and how much you made every year.

To be eligible for SSDI, you need to have paid into Social Security Administration which means if you were being paid via W2 your whole life you should have paid into this. If you were self-employed and did not pay into Social Security on your own, you will not have accumulated the working credits you need. Self-Employment is any work that was done, and they paid you in cash, 1099, or if you were a business owner.

1.4.2 Supplemental Security Income (SSI)

SSI is intended for individuals with limited income and resources, including those who may not have a substantial work history. It provides cash assistance to help meet basic needs such as food, clothing, and shelter. Eligibility for SSI is based on both financial need and disability status. To be eligible for SSI, you need to have less than $2,000 between a bank account, cash, and investments.

If you own a home, you must be living in it to be eligible, if you collect rent from renting an apartment in your home, this will be counted as income. You are allowed to own one vehicle, but any additional vehicle would be considered an asset and therefore, the value of vehicle will be counted in the amount of income they make their decision on. To be eligible for SSI, you need to be a United States Citizen and have proof of Citizenship Certificate if you are a naturalized alien.

1.5 Navigating the Complexity

Understanding the nuances of disability benefits can be overwhelming, but this guide is here to help you navigate the intricacies of the application process. As you move forward, remember that you have the right to seek assistance and explore your options. Some options are hiring an attorney or hiring an advocate. If you look for an advocate firm please keep in mind that you do not have to pay them up front, you would be signing a fee agreement that if your case is approved they will collect a certain percentage from the retroactive benefits which would be a one-time fee. Disability benefits can be a lifeline during a challenging time, and arming yourself with knowledge is the first step toward securing the support you need.

In the following chapters, we will explore how to gather the necessary documentation, determine which program is right for you, and guide you through the application process. Remember, you're not alone on this journey, and this guide is here to support you every step of the way.

Chapter 2: Gathering Important Information

One of the key factors in a successful disability benefits application is having the right information and documentation at your disposal. In this chapter, we'll explore the essential documents anc details you need to collect before starting your application process. Properly organizing and presenting this information can significantly improve the chances of a smoother application journey.

2.1 Understanding Documentation Needs

When applying for disability benefits, the Social Security Administration (SSA) will require detailed information about your medical condition, work history, and personal background. This documentation helps the SSA evaluate your eligibility and assess the impact of your disability on your ability to work.

2.2 Medical Records and Documentation

The cornerstone of your disability benefits application is your medical records. These records provide evidence of your medical condition, its severity, and its impact on your daily life. Some important medical documentation includes:

Diagnosis Records: Official records that confirm your medical condition from licensed medical professionals.

Treatment History: Documentation of treatments, medications, therapies, surgeries, and any medical interventions related to your condition.

Medical Test Results: Any medical tests, scans, or laboratory results that support your diagnosis.

Physician Statements: Statements from your doctors describing the nature and severity of your condition, as well as your functional limitations.

Hospitalization Records: Records of any hospitalizations, surgeries, or significant medical events related to your condition.

2.3 Work History Documentation

For Social Security Disability Insurance (SSDI) applications, your work history is an important factor in determining eligibility. Gather the following work-related documentation:

Social Security Statement: Obtain a copy of your Social Security Statement, which outlines your earnings history and estimates of future benefits. This can be found if you create an account on the SSA.gov website.

W-2 Forms: Collect W-2 forms from your past employers as proof of income.

Work History Details: Make a list of jobs you've held in the past 15 years, including job titles, responsibilities, and dates of employment.

Job Descriptions: Provide detailed descriptions of your job tasks, responsibilities, and any physical or mental demands required for each position.

2.4 Personal Information and Documentation

The SSA will also need personal information to verify your identity and process your application:

Immigration Status: A copy of green card or copy of Citizenship certificate.

Birth Certificate: A copy of your birth certificate to verify your age.

Social Security Number: Your Social Security number is essential for identity verification.

Marital Status: Information about your marital status, including spouse's name, Spouse's Social Security Number, date of marriage, and, if applicable, divorce records.

Dependent Information: If you have dependents, gather their names and Social Security numbers.

2.5 Organizing Your Documentation

Proper organization of your documentation can streamline the application process:

Create Folders: Organize documents into folders, separating medical records, work history, and personal information.

Label Clearly: Label folders clearly to quickly locate specific information when needed.

Make Copies: Create copies of all documents, as some may be required for multiple steps in the application process.

2.6 Maintaining Records

It's crucial to maintain copies of all documentation, as you may need them during various stages of the application, including appeals if necessary.

In the next chapter, we'll explore the eligibility criteria in more detail and help you determine whether you meet the SSA's definition of disability. Remember, gathering accurate and comprehensive documentation is a pivotal step toward a successful application for disability benefits.

Chapter 3: Determining Eligibility

Before diving into the application process for disability benefits, it's important to assess whether you meet the eligibility criteria set by the Social Security Administration (SSA). In this chapter, we'll explore the various components of eligibility and provide guidance on how to determine if you qualify for disability benefits.

3.1 Understanding the Key Criteria

The SSA's criteria for determining eligibility are based on several important factors. To be considered eligible for disability benefits, you must meet the following criteria:

Medical Condition: You must have a medically determinable impairment that prevents you from engaging in substantial gainful activity (SGA).
Inability to Work: Your medical condition must render you unable to perform your previous work or any other kind of substantial gainful activity.
Duration of Disability: Your disability must have lasted, or be expected to last, for at least 12 consecutive months or result in death.

3.2 Meeting the Definition of Disability

Central to your eligibility is whether your medical condition meets the SSA's definition of disability. The SSA defines disability as the inability to engage in substantial gainful activity (SGA) due to a medically determinable physical or mental impairment that can be expected to result in death or has lasted or is expected to last for a continuous period of at least 12 months.

3.3 Assessing Your Ability to Work

The SSA evaluates your ability to work based on the severity of your medical condition and its impact on your functional capacity. The assessment includes evaluating your physical and mental capabilities and determining whether you can perform your previous work or any other type of work. The SSA considers factors such as your age, education, skills, and work experience.

3.4 Gathering Medical Evidence

Strong medical evidence is essential for demonstrating the severity of your medical condition. The SSA will review medical records, doctor's reports, test results, and other documentation to assess the impact of your impairment on your ability to work. Be prepared to provide comprehensive medical documentation that clearly illustrates your condition's limitations.

3.5 Predicting Duration of Disability

It's important to assess whether your medical condition meets the duration requirement of at least 12 months. While you may not have a crystal-clear prediction of how long your disability will last, your medical professionals can provide insights based on their expertise.

3.6 Seeking Professional Guidance

Determining your eligibility can be complex, especially considering the medical and legal aspects involved. Consulting with a disability attorney or advocate can provide you with expert guidance in understanding the SSA's criteria and how they apply to your specific situation.

3.7 Self-Assessment of Eligibility

Before proceeding with the application process, conduct a self-assessment of your eligibility by evaluating your medical condition, its impact on your daily life, and your ability to work. Be honest and thorough in your evaluation to ensure that you have a clear understanding of whether you meet the SSA's eligibility criteria.

In the next chapter, we'll explore the two main disability benefit programs offered by the SSA: Social Security Disability Insurance (SSDI) and Supplemental Security Income (SSI). Understanding the differences between these programs will help you choose the one that aligns with your circumstances and needs. Remember, eligibility is the foundation upon which your disability benefits journey begins.

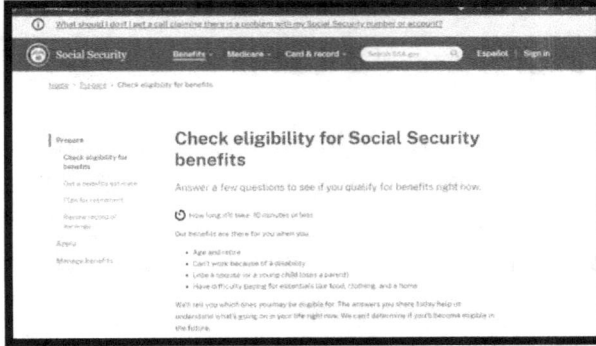

Chapter 4: Choosing the Right Program: SSDI vs. SSI

When applying for disability benefits through the Social Security Administration (SSA), it's important to understand the differences between the two main programs available: Social Security Disability Insurance (SSDI) and Supplemental Security Income (SSI). Each program has specific eligibility criteria and serves different purposes. In this chapter, we'll explore the distinctions between SSDI and SSI to help you determine which program aligns with your situation better, but you are able to apply for both if you qualify.

4.1 Social Security Disability Insurance (SSDI)
4.1.1 Eligibility Criteria
To be eligible for SSDI, you generally need to meet the following requirements:

- You have a significant work history and have earned sufficient work credits through payment of Social Security taxes.
- Your medical condition prevents you from engaging in substantial gainful activity (SGA).
- You meet the SSA's definition of disability.
- You have earned enough work credits within the timeframe specified by the SSA.

4.1.2 Benefit Calculation

Your SSDI benefit amount is based on your average lifetime earnings covered by Social Security. The more you've earned and contributed to Social Security during your working years, the higher your monthly benefit may be.

4.1.3 Medicare Eligibility

After receiving SSDI benefits for 24 months, you become eligible for Medicare coverage, which provides medical insurance to help cover healthcare expenses.

4.2 Supplemental Security Income (SSI)
4.2.1 Eligibility Criteria

SSI is designed to assist individuals with limited income and resources. To be eligible for SSI, you generally need to meet the following requirements:

- You have limited income and resources, including cash, real estate, or other assets. Bank account should be under $2k, you are able to own one property if you live in it. If you have life insurance, the cash value of your policy will be counted towards the assets.
- You meet the SSA's definition of disability.
- You are a U.S. citizen or meet certain immigration criteria.
- You are aged 65 or older, blind, or disabled.

4.2.2 Benefit Calculation

SSI benefits are determined by federal regulations and can vary based on your income, living arrangements, and other factors. In some cases, your state may supplement the federal SSI benefit with additional funds. The SSI monthly benefits usually rise from year to year to make sure you are able to afford the rising cost of living.

4.2.3 Medicaid Eligibility

Qualifying for SSI also grants you eligibility for Medicaid, a state-federal program that offers health coverage for eligible individuals with low income.

4.3 Choosing the Right Program for You
4.3.1 Considerations for SSDI

If you have a significant work history and have earned work credits, SSDI may be the appropriate program for you.
If your disability prevents you from working and you meet the eligibility criteria, SSDI can provide valuable financial support based on your past earnings.
4.3.2 Considerations for SSI

If you have limited income and resources, SSI may be the suitable program to help cover basic living expenses.
SSI can be particularly helpful for individuals with minimal or no work history.

4.3.3 Dual Eligibility

In some cases, you might be eligible for both SSDI and SSI, especially if your SSDI benefit amount is low due to limited work credits or if you have additional financial needs that SSI can address. To ensure you are filing for the correct benefits I would start with reviewing your earnings record, if it had an amount, you would receive if you became disabled, it means you are eligible. Now if that amount is under $800, I would file for both benefits just to make sure that if you are eligible for SSI based on the income, you would receive at least the maximum that SSI allows for the given year.

4.4 Making an Informed Choice

Choosing between SSDI and SSI requires careful consideration of your work history, financial situation, and disability status. Consulting with a disability advocate or attorney can provide personalized guidance based on your circumstances.

In the next chapter, we'll guide you through the process of actually applying for disability benefits, regardless of whether you're pursuing SSDI, SSI, or both. Remember, understanding the distinctions between these programs will help you make an informed decision that best meets your needs during this challenging time.

Chapter 5: The Application Process

Now that you have a clear understanding of disability benefits and the programs available, it's time to dive into the application process itself. In this chapter, we'll guide you through the steps to apply for disability benefits through the Social Security Administration (SSA), whether you're seeking Social Security Disability Insurance (SSDI) or Supplemental Security Income (SSI).

5.1 Preparing for the Application

Before you begin the application, take some time to gather all the necessary documentation and information you'll need. This includes medical records, work history details, personal identification, and any other relevant documents. Being organized from the start can save you time and reduce potential stress later in the process.

5.2 Online Application
5.2.1 Benefits of Applying Online

Applying for disability benefits online offers several advantages, including the ability to start and save your application, receive real-time status updates, and avoid long wait times on the phone or at a Social Security office.

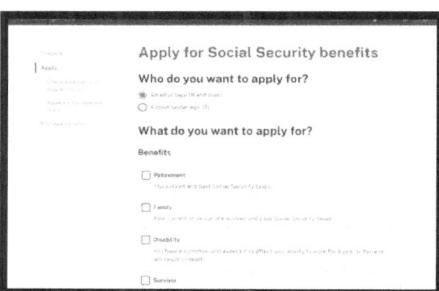

5.2.2 How to Apply Online

1. Visit the SSA Website: Go to the official Social Security Administration website (www.ssa.gov) and navigate to the "Apply for Disability Benefits" section.
2. Create an Account: If you don't have one already, create a "my Social Security" account to begin the application process.
3. Complete the Application: Follow the prompts to provide your personal information, work history, medical details, and other required information.
4. Upload Documentation: You'll have the opportunity to upload scanned copies of your medical records and other relevant documents.
5. Submit the Application: Review your application for accuracy and submit it electronically.

5.3 In-Person Application

If you prefer to apply in person or if you encounter technical difficulties with the online application, you can visit your local Social Security office to complete the process. To apply for SSI, you need to do application directly with Social Security, so you can call and make an appointment to go into the office or schedule a telephone appointment to complete application.

5.3.1 Scheduling an Appointment

It's recommended to schedule an appointment to avoid long wait times at the office. You can call the SSA or visit their website to set up an appointment.

5.3.2 What to Bring

When visiting the SSA office, bring all your prepared documentation, identification, and any other materials necessary for your application.

5.4 Phone Application

You can also apply for disability benefits over the phone by calling the SSA's toll-free number. If you want to search for the local Social Security office, you can do so by navigating to locating office on the SSA.gov website, where you will put your zip code and it will let you know what office you need to speak to.

5.4.1 Initiating the Phone Application

Call the SSA's toll-free number: 1-800-772-1213 (TTY 1-800-325-0778).
Follow the automated prompts to start your application.
During the call, you'll relate to a representative who will guide you through the application process. Be sure to have all your documentation and information ready to provide accurate responses.

5.5 What to Expect After Applying

After submitting your application, you'll receive confirmation of receipt. The SSA will then review your application and documentation to determine your eligibility. This process can take several months due to the high volume of applications. Typically for the initial application it takes anywhere from 4 to 6 months for a decision if offices are not backed up.

While waiting for a decision, you can use your "my Social Security" account to check the status of your application, receive updates, and communicate with the SSA.

In the next chapter, we'll delve into the importance of strong medical evidence and documentation to support your disability benefits application. Remember, each step you take brings you closer to potentially receiving the support you need during this challenging time.

Chapter 6: Medical Evidence and Documentation

A crucial aspect of a successful disability benefits application is the presentation of strong and comprehensive medical evidence. In this chapter, we'll delve into the importance of medical documentation, how to gather and organize it, and strategies to present your medical case effectively to the Social Security Administration (SSA).

6.1 The Role of Medical Evidence

Medical evidence serves as the foundation of your disability claim. It provides objective information that supports the severity of your medical condition and its impact on your ability to work. The more thorough and detailed your medical evidence, the stronger your case will be. Make sure that when filing the online application you list all doctors you have seen with their correct contact information such as clinic name, address, and phone number as this will be used to request your medical information.

6.2 Gathering Medical Records

Collecting your medical records is a critical step. These records should reflect your medical history, diagnoses, treatments, medications, surgeries, and any other relevant information related to your condition. Reach out to your healthcare providers, specialists, and hospitals to request copies of your medical records. Social Security Administration will be sending your application to the Disability Determination Office and this office will assign an adjudicator who will request your medical records so please do not pay too much money trying to acquire your records on your own. The only way I would suggest that you pay for the copy of your medical records, is if your medical provider is not responding to the medical records request DDS is sending them.

6.3 Doctor's Statements and Reports

Statements from your treating physicians and specialists can provide valuable insights into the nature and limitations of your medical condition. These statements should detail your diagnosis, symptoms, treatments, and functional limitations. If possible, request that your doctors include information about your ability to perform physical and mental tasks related to work. Keep in mind that although your doctor states that you are disabled in the statement, Social Security Administration will make their own decision based on the medical evidence itself.

6.4 Medical Tests and Imaging

Any medical tests, imaging results, laboratory reports, and diagnostic studies that support your diagnosis should be included in your documentation. This could include X-rays, MRIs, blood tests, and other relevant medical assessments.

6.5 Functional Assessments

Functional assessments evaluate your ability to perform various physical and mental tasks. They provide an objective measure of your limitations and are particularly important if your condition affects your ability to work. Your doctor's assessment of your ability to stand, walk, lift, carry, concentrate, and interact socially can significantly influence your case. The office of Disability Determinations will sometimes send your doctor functional assessments to complete.

6.6 Consistency and Continuity

Ensure that your medical evidence is consistent across all documents. Any inconsistencies or gaps could raise doubts about the severity of your condition. Regular visits to your healthcare providers can also help maintain the continuity of your medical records. The easiest way to understand this, is to assume that if you are really disabled and unable to work any job, that you would be seeing doctors regularly regarding your severe medical conditions.

6.7 Organizing Your Medical Documentation

Organize your medical evidence in a clear and logical manner. Create folders for different aspects of your medical history, diagnoses, treatments, and assessments. Label folders and documents clearly so that they are easily accessible when needed. I would suggest making a list of all the conditions you have been diagnosed with and also keep a track of what doctor gave the diagnosis.

6.8 Quality over Quantity

While comprehensive medical evidence is essential, the quality of the documentation matters more than the quantity. Focus on obtaining detailed reports and statements that provide a clear understanding of your condition's impact on your daily life and ability to work.

6.9 Seek Specialist Opinions

If your medical condition is complex and involves multiple specialists, consider seeking opinions from experts in the relevant fields. Specialist opinions can add credibility to your case and provide a more complete understanding of your condition. If you have multiple conditions and are only seeing a primary care doctor, please ask them to give you referrals to specialists because a primary care doctor's opinion does not hold much weight with Social Security Administration.

6.10 Relevance and Currency

Ensure that your medical evidence is current and relevant. Recent documentation that accurately reflects your current medical status is more persuasive than outdated records.

6.11 Review and Consultation

Before submitting your application, review your medical documentation thoroughly. If possible, consult with a disability attorney or advocate to ensure that your medical evidence effectively supports your claim.

In the next chapter, we'll explore the documentation related to your work history and income, which is particularly important for Social Security Disability Insurance (SSDI) applications. Remember, well-organized and comprehensive medical evidence can significantly enhance your chances of a successful disability benefits application.

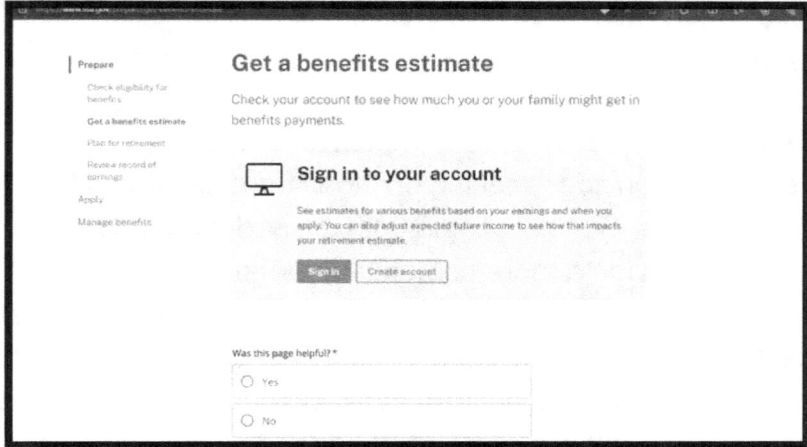

Chapter 7: Work History and Income Documentation

When applying for disability benefits, especially for Social Security Disabi ity Insurance (SSDI), your work history and income play a crucial role in establishing eligibility. In this chapter, we'll discuss the significance of work history and income documentation, how to gather the necessary information, and the ways in which they impact your disability benefits application.

7.1 The Importance of Work History

For SSDI applications, your work history is a key factor in determining eligibility. The Social Security Administration (SSA) uses work cred ts to assess whether you've paid enough into the system to q ualify for benefits. Work credits are earned based on your yearly income and the amount of Social Security taxes you've paid.

7.2 Gathering Work History Information

Gather detailed information about your work history, including job titles, responsibilities, employers' names, dates of employment, and earnings. For the initial application, you only need work histcry for the last ten years. Consider the following steps:

Review your Social Security Statement, which provides a summary of your earnings history and work credits.
Collect W-2 forms, tax returns, and other documents that show your annual earnings.

7.3 Earning Work Credits

Work credits are earned by accumulating a specific amount of income subject to Social Security taxes. The number of credits required for SSDI eligibility varies based on your age when you become disabled. For instance, a younger person might need fewer credits compared to an older individual.

7.4 Calculating Eligibility

To determine whether you have enough work credits to be eligible for SSDI, consult your Social Security Statement or contact the SSA. If you're unsure about your eligibility based on work credits, consider consulting a disability advocate or attorney.

7.5 Income Documentation for SSI

For Supplemental Security Income (SSI) applications, your income is a crucial consideration. SSI benefits are determined based on financial need, so accurate income documentation is essential. Income includes money you earn from work, as well as non-work sources such as pensions, alimony, and public assistance.

7.6 Reporting Changes in Income

It's important to report any changes in your income to the SSA. This includes changes in wages, pensions, or other sources of income. Failing to report changes could result in incorrect benefit calculations or overpayments.

7.7 Assets and Resources for SSI

In addition to income, the SSA also considers your resources (assets) when determining SSI eligibility. Resources include cash, bank accounts, real estate (other than your primary residence), and personal property that could be converted to cash.

7.8 Reviewing and Verifying Income Documentation

Before submitting your application, carefully review your income and work history documentation for accuracy. Any inconsistencies or errors could lead to delays in processing your application.

7.9 Consultation and Assistance

If you're unsure about how to gather and document your work history and income, consider seeking assistance from a disability advocate, attorney, or the SSA itself. Accurate and complete documentation is essential for a successful disability benefits application.

In the next chapter, we'll guide you through the actual application process, discussing the steps you'll need to take to submit your application to the Social Security Administration. Remember, proper documentation of your work history and income will help ensure that you present a strong case for disability benefits eligibility.

Chapter 8: The Waiting Period and Decision

After you've submitted your disability benefits application to the Social Security Administration (SSA), a waiting period begins before you receive a decision on your eligibility. In this chapter, we'll explore what to expect during this waiting period, the factors that influence the decision-making process, and the different possible outcomes of your application.

8.1 The Waiting Period

Once your application is submitted, the SSA will review your documentation, medical evidence, work history, and income details. The waiting period for a decision can vary, but it often takes several months due to the volume of applications and the thoroughness of the review process. It typically takes anywhere from four to six months to receive a decision.

8.2 Medical Review and Evaluation

During the waiting period, the SSA will closely examine your medical records and evidence to determine the severity of your condition and its impact on your ability to work. They may request additional medical information or evaluations if needed. Once an adjudicator is assigned to your case, you will receive in the mail two forms to fill out which include an Adult Function Report, and a Work History Report. These two forms need to be filled out in order for them to be able to make a medical decision on your case, failure to submit will result in a denial. Also, at this point you can follow up with the adjudicator to make sure that all your medical records were obtained.

8.3 Consultative Examinations

In some cases, the SSA might schedule a consultative examination with a healthcare provider contracted by the SSA. This additional evaluation is designed to provide more information about your medical condition. These exams are paid by SSA, which means if you fail to attend once and it is rescheduled and you still do not attend, it is an automatic denial. The reason for this is because they have to pay the doctors whether you show up for the exam or not.

8.4 The Decision

After thoroughly reviewing your application and supporting documentation, the SSA will make a decision on your eligibility for disability benefits. There are three possible outcomes:

Approval: If the SSA determines that you meet the eligibility criteria and the severity of your medical condition prevents you from engaging in substantial gainful activity, your application will be approved.

Denial: If the SSA finds that you do not meet the eligibility criteria or that your medical condition does not meet the required level of severity, your application will be denied. Denials can occur for various reasons, including insufficient medical evidence or inconsistencies in your documentation.

Further Evaluation: In some cases, the SSA might need more information to make a decision. This could involve additional medical evaluations or clarification on specific aspects of your application.

8.5 Receiving the Decision

You will receive a written notice of the SSA's decision by mail. If your application is approved, the notice will outline the number of benefits you'll receive and when they will begin. If you applied for SSI, before an approval letter is sent out, they will contact you by phone to do an income review which is mandatory for this type of benefit. If your application is denied, the notice will explain the reasons for the denial and provide information on how to appeal the decision.

8.6 Appeals and Reconsideration

If your application is denied, you have the right to appeal the decision. Appeals can be filed online as well which ensures that SSA receives the appeal within the time frame given which is 60 days from the date on the denial letter. The appeals process involves requesting a reconsideration, where your case will be reviewed by a different SSA examiner. If the reconsideration is also denied, you can request a hearing before an administrative law judge.

8.7 Staying Informed

During the waiting period, you can use your "my Social Security" account to check the status of your application and receive updates. This account also provides access to information about your benefits and other relevant details.

<u>8.8 Managing Expectations</u>

It's important to have realistic expectations during the waiting period. While it can be challenging to wait for a decision, the thorough review process ensures that each application receives proper consideration.

In the next chapter, we'll delve into the appeals and reconsideration process for denied applications. Remember, the waiting period is an integral part of the application journey, and staying informed and patient is key to navigating this stage successfully.

Chapter 9: Appeals and Reconsideration

Receiving a denial of your disability benefits application from the Social Security Administration (SSA) is not the end of the road. The appeals process provides you with the opportunity to challenge the decision and present additional evidence to support your case. In this chapter, we'll guide you through the appeals and reconsideration process, helping you understand your options after a denial.

<u>9.1 Understanding the Need for Appeals</u>

If your disability benefits application is denied, it's important to remember that denials are not uncommon. Many applications are initially denied due to various factors, including incomplete documentation or misinterpretation of medical evidence. The appeals process is designed to provide a fair opportunity for you to present your case again.

9.2 Initiating an Appeal

The first step in the appeals process is to request a reconsideration. To do this, follow these steps:

Review the Denial Notice: Carefully read the denial notice you received from the SSA. It will outline the reasons for the denial and provide instructions on how to appeal. If any medical providers did not send in your medical records, I would suggest you contact them and have them release the medical records directly to you, so that you can upload them with the appeal or send them to the adjudicator once the case is sent back for a second medical decision.

Request a Reconsideration: Fill out the appropriate forms or follow the online process to request a reconsideration. You'll need to provide additional information, evidence, and documentation to support your case. I would suggest you do the online appeal versus paper forms, because the paper appeals sometimes get lost in the mail or they do not get processed on time at the local field office.

Deadline: Ensure that you file your request for reconsideration within the specified deadline, typically 60 days from the date of the denial notice.

9.3 Gathering Additional Evidence

During the reconsideration process, you have the opportunity to submit new medical evidence, updated documentation, and any other relevant information that strengthens your case. This is your chance to address the reasons for the initial denial and present a more comprehensive picture of your disability and its impact on your life.

9.4 Reconsideration Decision

After submitting your appeal, the SSA will conduct a thorough review of your case, including the new evidence you've provided. They will issue a reconsideration decision, which can result in one of the following outcomes:

Approval: If the SSA determines that your additional evidence supports your eligibility for disability benefits, your application will be approved.

Denial: If the SSA still finds that you do not meet the eligibility criteria or that the new evidence is insufficient to change their decision, your appeal will be denied.

9.5 Moving Forward: Further Appeals

If your request for reconsideration is denied, you have the option to continue appealing. The next step involves requesting a hearing before an administrative law judge. This hearing allows you to present your case in person and provide additional evidence and testimony.

9.6 Seeking Legal Representation

As the appeals process becomes more complex, you might consider seeking legal representation or assistance from a disability attorney or advocate. At this level, you should perhaps look into seeking legal representation as preparing for a hearing takes a lot of work. If you want to continue on your own, it is fine, but you need to make sure all your medical records are up to date in your file.

They can provide expert guidance, help you gather compelling evidence, and navigate the appeals process more effectively.

At the hearing level, the timespan to receive a hearing date varies as they are scheduling telephone hearings much faster than in person hearings. Due Covid-19 they started doing telephone hearings, whether this is an option at the time you file an appeal to request a hearing date, I suggest doing an in person hearing where the judge will be able to see you in person and see the physical limitations you might have.

<u>9.7 Persistence and Patience</u>

The appeals process can be lengthy, but persistence is key. Keep in mind that many individuals who are initially denied eventually receive approval through the appeals process. Stay patient, gather strong evidence, and remain committed to securing the benefits you deserve.

In the next chapter, we'll explore the administrative hearing process for appeals, providing insights into what to expect during the hearing and how to prepare effectively. Remember, the appeals process is your opportunity to advocate for yourself and present a comprehensive case for disability benefits eligibility.

Chapter 10: Navigating the Administrative Process

As you navigate the appeals process for your disability benefits application, the possibility of an administrative hearing may arise. This stage provides you with the chance to present your case in person before an administrative law judge. In this chapter, we'll delve into what to expect during an administrative hearing, how to prepare, and what options you have if the hearing outcome is not favorable.

10.1 The Administrative Hearing Process

An administrative hearing is a formal proceeding where you have the opportunity to present your case and provide testimony in person before an administrative law judge. This stage comes after your request for reconsideration is denied and you've appealed for further review.

10.2 Preparing for the Hearing
10.2.1 Gathering Evidence

Before the hearing, gather all relevant medical records, documentation, and evidence that support your disability claim. This includes medical reports, treatment records, statements from doctors, and any other materials that demonstrate the impact of your condition on your ability to work. Do not get copies of medical records that Social Security Administration already has, get up to date medical records instead. Also, you can call the hearings office and request to be sent a cd with all your case information if you plan on representing yourself at the hearing.

10.2.2 Testimony and Witnesses

Prepare a clear and concise statement that describes your medical condition, its severity, and its impact on your daily life and ability to work. You may also want to bring witnesses who can testify about your condition and limitations. These witnesses could include family members, friends, or coworkers.

10.2.3 Legal Representation

Consider seeking legal representation for the administrative hearing. A disability attorney or advocate can help you navigate the hearing process, prepare your case effectively, and provide expert guidance. I highly suggest seeking legal representation at this level as an attorney or advocate will be able to argue against any job recommendations that are brought up by the vocational expert at the hearing.

10.3 The Hearing Procedure
10.3.1 Opening Statements

The hearing typically begins with an opening statement from the administrative law judge, where they outline the purpose of the hearing and explain the process.

10.3.2 Presentation of Evidence

You and your representative (if you have one) will have the opportunity to present evidence, including medical records, documentation, and testimony. The judge may ask questions to clarify your statements.

10.3.3 Witnesses

If you've brought witnesses, they will be asked to provide testimony about your condition, limitations, and any other relevant information.

10.3.4 Cross-Examination

The judge or the representative from the SSA may ask you and your witnesses questions to further clarify the evidence presented. A vocational expert will also provide the judge with any jobs you may be able to do based on your conditions, limitations, previous work experience and education.

10.3.5 Closing Statements

After all the evidence and the testimony has been presented, both you and the SSA representative (if present) will have the chance to make closing statements summarizing your case.

10.4 The Hearing Decision

After the administrative hearing, the judge will review the evidence and testimony presented and make a decision regarding your eligibility for disability benefits. This decision will be mailed to you, outlining the judge's findings and rationale.

10.5 Possible Outcomes

The outcomes of an administrative hearing can vary:

Approval: If the judge finds that you meet the eligibility criteria for disability benefits, your application will be approved. If it is approved, expect to receive two letters, one from the hearings office outlining the approval from the judge and one from the Social Security Administration local office letting you know you were approved and how much your monthly benefits will be and if there is any retro active payment.

Denial: If the judge determines that you do not meet the eligibility criteria, your application will be denied.

10.6 If the Outcome Is Unfavorable

If your application is denied after the administrative hearing, you still have options:

Appeal to the Appeals Council: You can request that the Social Security Appeals Council review your case if you believe the judge's decision was incorrect or unjust. Filing for Appeals Council does not have a timespan so if you are desperately in need of benefits, I would refile instead of appealing but again it depends on various factors. If you were denied based on SSDI and your date last insured has passed, you should appeal because once you are denied at the hearing level there is no way for them to make another medical decision on the same time span.

Federal Court Review: If the Appeals Council denies your appeal or doesn't take up your case, you have the option to file a lawsuit in federal district court. Filing for federal district court should only be done if there were technical errors within the hearing process.

10.7 Staying Informed and Prepared

Navigating the administrative hearing stage requires thorough preparation, strong evidence, and effective communication. Consulting with a disability attorney or advocate can significantly enhance your chances of success.

In the final chapter, we'll provide a summary of key takeaways and tips to help you navigate the entire disability benefits application process. Remember, an administrative hearing is a significant opportunity to present your case directly, so thorough preparation is essential.

Chapter 11: Additional Resources and Support

Congratulations on reaching the end of this comprehensive guide to applying for disability benefits through the Social Security Administration (SSA). Navigating the process of seeking assistance for your disability can be complex, but armed with the right information and strategies, you're better equipped to face the challenges. In this final chapter, we'll summarize the key takeaways and offer some last-minute tips to help you successfully navigate the disability benefits application journey.

11.1 Key Takeaways

Understand Eligibility: Familiarize yourself with the eligibility criteria for the different disability benefit programs, such as Social Security Disability Insurance (SSDI) and Supplemental Security Income (SSI).

Gather Comprehensive Documentation: Thoroughly collect and organize your medical records, work history, income documentation, and any other evidence that supports your disability claim.

Be Accurate and Honest: Provide accurate and truthful information throughout the application process. Inaccuracies can lead to delays or denials.

Seek Professional Guidance: Consider consulting a disability attorney or advocate to navigate the complexities of the application and appeals processes.

Be Patient: The application process can be lengthy. Maintain patience and persistence, knowing that many applicants eventually receive benefits after the appeals process. Initial process can take about 4 to 6 months. If denied you can appeal within 60 days for a reconsideration. At the reconsideration level, the timespan is anywhere from 1 to 3 months for a decision. If denied, appeal for a hearing request and at the hearing level it can take over 12 months from the appeal date to have a hearing and get a decision.

Prepare for the Appeals Process: Understand that denials are common, and the appeals process provides you with opportunities to strengthen your case.

Appeal Deadlines: Pay close attention to deadlines for filing appeals or requests for reconsideration. Missing deadlines can impact your chances of success.

11.2 Final Tips

Stay Organized: Keep all your documentation organized and easily accessible throughout the entire process.

Keep Copies: Always make copies of any documents you submit, as you may need them for reference during the appeals process.

Maintain Open Communication: If you move or your contact information changes, notify the SSA promptly to ensure you receive important correspondence.

Utilize Online Resources: The SSA website provides valuable resources, forms, and information related to disability benefits. Utilize their online tools to stay informed.

Use Your "my Social Security" Account: Create an account to track your application, receive updates, and access important documents.

Seek Support: Don't hesitate to reach out to family, friends, or support groups for emotional and practical assistance during the application process.

Be Persistent: Remember that the disability benefits application journey can be challenging. Stay committed to advocating for yourself and your needs.

<u>11.3 Moving Forward</u>

As you embark on your disability benefits journey, remember that you're not alone. Many individuals have successfully navigated this process and received the assistance they need. Each step you take brings you closer to potential financial support that can alleviate some of the burdens caused by your disability.

Whether your application is approved at the initial stage or requires appeals, remember that your determination and commitment to providing accurate and comprehensive documentation can significantly impact your chances of success. Best of luck as you navigate this journey toward securing the benefits you deserve!

Conclusion : Navigating Your Path to Disability Benefits

In the journey of life, unexpected challenges can arise, and sometimes these challenges lead us to seek assistance. Navigating the path to disability benefits through the Social Security Administration (SSA) is a significant undertaking, but armed with knowledge, preparation, and persistence, you can navigate this complex process with confidence.

Throughout this eBook, we've explored the ins and outs of applying for disability benefits, from understanding eligibility criteria to gathering compelling evidence, from submitting your application to potentially appealing denials. Remember that the journey is not always straightforward, but every step you take brings you closer to the financial support you need to manage the impact of your disability.

As you move forward, keep in mind the importance of staying organized, seeking professional guidance when needed, and maintaining open communication with the SSA. Remember that denials are not the end; they are often a starting point for appeals that allow you to present your case more comprehensively.

Your journey to disability benefits is a journey of empowerment. It's about advocating for your rights, seeking the support you deserve, and demonstrating the value of your unique experiences. Embrace each stage with determination, knowing that you are not alone in this process.

Your perseverance is admirable, and your commitment to securing the assistance you need is a testament to your strength. The path might be challenging, but the potential rewards are invaluable. Whether your application is approved at the initial stage or requires appeals, know that your efforts matter, and they can make a significant difference in your life.

Remember that this eBook serves as a guide, providing insights and guidance to help you navigate the disability benefits application process. As you continue on your journey, never hesitate to seek support, both from those around you and from professionals who specialize in disability benefits cases.

Your story is unique, and your journey is one of resilience. We wish you the best of luck as you navigate the path to disability benefits, and we hope that this eBook has equipped you with the information and tools you need to face this challenge with confidence.

Stay strong, stay informed, and stay committed to securing the benefits that can help you achieve a better quality of life. Your journey is an inspiring one, and we believe in your ability to succeed.

Warmest wishes on your journey to securing the support you deserve.

Sincerely,

Maria Gonzalez